GRAND CANYON
National Park

by Ashley Storm

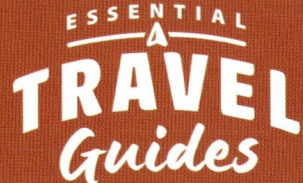

An Imprint of Abdo Publishing
abdobooks.com

ABDOBOOKS.COM

Published by Abdo Publishing, a division of ABDO, PO Box 398166, Minneapolis, Minnesota 55439. Copyright © 2026 by Abdo Consulting Group, Inc. International copyrights reserved in all countries. No part of this book may be reproduced in any form without written permission from the publisher. Essential Library™ is a trademark and logo of Abdo Publishing.

Printed in China.
052025
092025

THIS BOOK CONTAINS RECYCLED MATERIALS

Cover Photo: Kristina Bilous/Shutterstock Images
Interior Photos: Amanda Mohler/Shutterstock Images, 4–5; Joe Belanger/Shutterstock Images, 7; Shutterstock Images, 9, 66–67, 72, 77, 82, 89; Natural History Archive/Alamy, 12, 48; Felicia Fonseca/AP Images, 15; Michael Quinn/National Park Service, 16–17, 24; H. Mark Weidman Photography/Alamy, 18–19; Allison Bailey/Alamy, 22–23; Moritz Wolf/imageBROKER.com/Alamy, 26–27; Peter Unger/Stone/Getty Images, 30, 36; John Elk/The Image Bank Unreleased/Getty Images, 33; Nature and Science/Alamy, 35; Arterra/Universal Images Group/Getty Images, 38–39; Marianne A. Campolongo/Alamy, 41; Diana Robinson Photography/Moment/Getty Images, 44; Udo Siebig/mauritius images GmbH/Alamy, 47; Christopher Babcock/Shutterstock Images, 51; Thomas Blanck/Shutterstock Images, 52–53; Alex Fairweather/Alamy, 56; Patrick J. Endres/Corbis Documentary/Getty Images, 59; Francisco Blanco/Shutterstock Images, 62; Travis J. Camp/Shutterstock Images, 64–65; Mark Meredith/Moment Unreleased/Getty Images, 69; Layne V. Naylor/Shutterstock Images, 74; Rodrigo Abd/AP Images, 78–79; Ron Buskirk/UCG/Universal Images Group/Getty Images, 83; Charton Franck/hemis.fr/Alamy, 84–85; Markus Lange/mauritius images GmbH/Alamy, 90–91; Jim West/Alamy, 92; Maj. Erin Hannigan/US Army/AP Images, 95; Gordon Montgomery/Shutterstock Images, 98; Red Line Editorial, 101

Editor: Laura Stickney
Series Designer: Joshua Olson

Library of Congress Control Number: 2024948600

PUBLISHER'S CATALOGING-IN-PUBLICATION DATA

Names: Storm, Ashley, author.
Title: Grand Canyon National Park / by Ashley Storm
Description: Minneapolis, Minnesota: Abdo Publishing, 2026 | Series: Essential travel guides | Includes online resources and index.
Identifiers: ISBN 9781098297107 (lib. bdg.) | ISBN 9798384919629 (ebook)
Subjects: LCSH: Grand Canyon National Park (Ariz.)--Juvenile literature. | Travel--Juvenile literature. | United States--Guidebooks--Juvenile literature. | National parks and reserves--Juvenile literature. | Historic sites--Juvenile literature.
Classification: DDC 917.91--dc23

CONTENTS

CHAPTER ONE
A NATIONAL TREASURE 4

CHAPTER TWO
GEOLOGICAL HISTORY 16

CHAPTER THREE
THE SOUTH RIM 26

CHAPTER FOUR
MAGNIFICENT VIEWS 38

CHAPTER FIVE
INTO THE CANYON 52

CHAPTER SIX
THE NORTH RIM 66

CHAPTER SEVEN
THE PEOPLE OF THE GRAND CANYON 78

CHAPTER EIGHT
STAYING SAFE 90

ESSENTIAL FACTS 100
GLOSSARY 102
ADDITIONAL RESOURCES 104
SOURCE NOTES 106
INDEX 110
ABOUT THE AUTHOR 112

CHAPTER
ONE

A NATIONAL TREASURE

The Grand Canyon, which stretches across northern Arizona, is a sight to behold. It is 18 miles (29 km) wide at its widest point and 6,000 feet (1,830 m) deep at its deepest point. It extends for 277 miles (446 km).[1] The canyon is so massive that it can even be seen from space. From that high up, the canyon looks like a big crack in the planet's surface.

With layers of red rock exposed by millions of years of erosion, the Grand Canyon serves as a time capsule for Earth. Its canyon walls showcase two billion years of geological history.[2] This close-up view of Earth's past, combined with the area's natural beauty and its wide range of activities for visitors of all ages, makes the Grand Canyon one of the most popular

Grand Canyon National Park covers more than 1.2 million acres (485,623 ha). It is the eleventh-largest national park in the United States.

tourist destinations in the world. Whether visitors prefer gazing at the view from the canyon's rim, rafting on the raging rapids of the Colorado River, or exploring the canyon by foot, bike, or mule, there's something for everyone at Grand Canyon National Park.

Conquistadors Reach the Canyon

For thousands of years, the Grand Canyon had few visitors other than the Indigenous peoples who called it their home. In the 1500s, Spanish explorer Francisco Vázquez de Coronado and his conquistadors were traveling north from what is now Mexico City, Mexico. They were searching for the legendary Seven Cities of Cibola, which they believed were cities of gold filled with treasure and riches.

One of Coronado's men, García López de Cárdenas, led a group of conquistadors farther into what is now the state of Arizona. In 1540, these men became the first Europeans to reach the Grand Canyon, encountering a Hopi settlement near the site. A Hopi guide took the conquistadors to the canyon's rim and pointed out

> "The Grand Canyon fills me with awe. It is beyond comparison—beyond description.[3]
> —President Theodore Roosevelt, on visiting the Grand Canyon in 1903

▲ Historians are unsure exactly where García López de Cárdenas and his men first saw the Grand Canyon. But most believe it was at the South Rim near Moran Point, *pictured*.

the Colorado River at the bottom of the canyon. From the rim, the conquistadors thought it looked like a river they could use to navigate to the Gulf of California, which is on Mexico's northwestern coast, and to the Pacific Ocean.

The conquistadors attempted to make their way down into the canyon. But they realized the river was not as narrow and calm as it appeared from above. It was too treacherous for travel, so the conquistadors left the area.

More than 200 years passed before other expedition groups ventured into the Grand Canyon area. Later, Mexico and the United States fought each other in the

Mexican-American War (1846–1848). The United States won the war. As part of the peace negotiations, Mexico ceded more than 500,000 square miles (1.3 million sq km) of its territory to the United States.[4] This included land that later became several states, including California, Nevada, Utah, New Mexico, and parts of Colorado and Arizona. The Grand Canyon region was part of this acquired territory. This made it an official part of the United States.

Early Tourism

In the late 1800s, a railroad was constructed to transport goods from Chicago, Illinois, to Los Angeles, California. The railroad passed through Arizona. Prospectors began to settle around the Grand Canyon area, hoping to mine for copper and gold there. Before long, they realized that tourism to the scenic area would be an even more

The Great Unknown

To most Americans in the mid-1800s, the Grand Canyon was a wild, unexplored area that many people referred to as "the Great Unknown." Most maps left the entire area blank. The only thing people knew for sure was that the Colorado River ran through the canyon. In 1857, the US government funded an expedition led by US Army first lieutenant Joseph Christmas Ives. The expedition's goal was to map the Colorado River and determine its usefulness as a trade route. Ives wrote that the "extent and magnitude of the system of canyons is astounding." But he concluded that the Grand Canyon was "altogether valueless" for trade or settlement.[5]

lucrative endeavor. Traveling by railroad was significantly faster and less expensive than crossing the country by stagecoach, allowing more people to visit the western United States than ever before.

To help facilitate tourism, the Grand Canyon Railway was built to bring visitors from Williams, Arizona, directly to the Grand Canyon. Williams is located in northern Arizona, about 60 miles (97 km) south of the canyon's South Rim.[6] The railway began transporting tourists to the canyon in 1901. The journey took about three hours.[7] Visitors were mesmerized by the canyon's beauty.

The Grand Canyon Railway first arrived at the canyon on September 17, 1901. Today, visitors can see an old-fashioned steam locomotive at Williams Depot.

Before long, adventurous visitors began trekking into the canyon. Some rafted on the Colorado River. Early visitors often camped at the canyon in tents. Developers quickly built hotels and restaurants in the area to accommodate the tourists.

Among the early entrepreneurs at the Grand Canyon were brothers Emery and Ellsworth Kolb. They were photographers who took pictures of the Grand Canyon and its visitors. The brothers opened a studio called Kolb Studio. They documented their river rafting adventures through the Grand Canyon on film.

Later, the Kolbs began traveling across the United States to share the wonder and beauty of the Grand Canyon with others. Through public talks, the brothers promoted tourism to the site. Today, Kolb Studio serves as an art gallery, museum, and bookstore.

All Aboard

As automobiles became the main mode of transportation for visitors to the Grand Canyon, fewer tourists used the Grand Canyon Railway. It closed to passengers in 1968 but reopened in 1989 as a tourist attraction. The steam railway cars were restored to their former glory. Today, the train runs daily from Williams, Arizona, to the Grand Canyon's South Rim. Visitors have the opportunity to experience the train as if they were among the earliest visitors to the national park. Entertainment on the train includes cowboy serenades. Passengers can also watch a Wild West shoot-out re-enactment at the Williams Depot train station.

Becoming a National Park

In 1882, US senator Benjamin Harrison filed a bill to designate "a certain tract of land lying on the Colorado River of the West in the Territory of Arizona as a public park."[8] At this time, few people had visited the Grand Canyon, so Harrison did not have the support of his fellow congressmen. The bill did not pass. Harrison tried to pass similar bills in 1883 and 1886, but neither succeeded.

However, Harrison was committed to conserving the wilderness of the United States, and he never gave up on trying to preserve the canyon for future generations. Harrison would later become US president, serving from 1889 to 1893. During his final weeks in office, Harrison used his executive powers to establish the Grand Canyon Forest Reserve. This protected the area's forests.

In 1903, US president Theodore Roosevelt visited the Grand Canyon. He was impressed by the beauty and grandeur of the rugged landscape. He famously declared the Grand Canyon to be "one of the great sights which every American . . . should see" and said it was "absolutely unparalleled throughout the rest of the world."[9] In 1906, Roosevelt issued a proclamation establishing the Grand Canyon National Game Preserve. This protected wild game animals in the area.

⚠ **Theodore Roosevelt,** *bottom left,* **was photographed on Bright Angel Trail during a 1911 visit to the Grand Canyon.**

Two years later, Roosevelt went further. He used his authority granted by the Antiquities Act of 1906. This gave the president the power to designate landmarks, historical sites, and other public lands as national monuments. Roosevelt used this power to name the Grand Canyon a national monument. He said the designation was due to the canyon's "unusual scientific interest, being the greatest eroded canyon within the United States."[10]

Only the US Congress can create an official national park, and it was another 11 years before the Grand Canyon received that designation. When Arizona became a state in 1912, one of its first senators was Henry Fountain Ashurst. Ashurst's father had been a prospector and miner in the Grand Canyon. In 1917, Ashurst introduced a bill that would lead to the creation of Grand Canyon National Park.

The United States' involvement in World War I (1914–1918) temporarily stalled the bill's progress. But it was finally passed by Congress and signed by President Woodrow Wilson in 1919. Later, in 1975, President Gerald Ford signed a law that doubled the park's size. This law established the current boundaries of Grand Canyon National Park.

Teddy the Conservationist President

President Theodore "Teddy" Roosevelt is known for his conservation efforts. He was passionate about preserving the wilderness of the United States for future generations. He doubled the number of national parks while he was in office. In 1902, Roosevelt was on a bear hunt in Mississippi. Members of his hunting party captured a bear and tied it to a tree so Roosevelt could easily kill it. The president refused, declaring it to be unsportsmanlike to kill a captive animal. Later, a toymaker created a stuffed bear called a Teddy Bear in Roosevelt's honor. It remains a popular toy today.

Indigenous Peoples of the Grand Canyon

Some areas of the Grand Canyon are not official parts of the national park. These areas are tribal lands. When Grand Canyon National Park was created, the US government forced

Indigenous peoples living in the region to make new homes in designated areas called reservations. The Diné (Navajo), Southern Paiute, and Hualapai peoples now live along the canyon's rim. The Hopi, Zuni, and Apache tribes are not far from the Grand Canyon. Today, the only Indigenous peoples who still live inside the Grand Canyon beneath the rim are the Havasupai.

The Havasupai lived in the Grand Canyon for more than 1,000 years before the creation of Grand Canyon National Park. In the 1970s, the Havasupai pushed for a congressional bill that would return some of their land to them. In 1975, they were victorious. Some reservation land along the South Rim was returned to the Havasupai.

Today, many reservations are located in or near the canyon. Some open their land to tourists. They offer a firsthand look at American Indian cultures of the region.

UNESCO World Heritage Site

In 1979, the Grand Canyon was recognized for its natural and cultural significance. It was named a United Nations Educational, Scientific and Cultural Organization (UNESCO) World Heritage site. To be named a UNESCO World Heritage site, prospective sites must go through a vigorous nomination process. The sites must meet

▲ In 2023, Havasupai members Dianna Sue Uqualla, Kris Siyuja, and Uqualla, *left to right*, performed a ceremonial blessing at the Havasupai Gardens campground in Grand Canyon National Park.

very strict criteria. It's not easy to be named to the prestigious list. The Grand Canyon's inclusion makes it a desirable tourist destination for both international and American visitors.

More than 100 years have passed since the Grand Canyon became a national park. The site's popularity continues to grow. Today, more than six million people visit the Grand Canyon every year.[11]

CHAPTER
TWO

GEOLOGICAL HISTORY

The Grand Canyon has a rich geological history. Many people gaze upon the magnificent grandeur of the Grand Canyon, marveling at its existence. They wonder how the canyon formed and what forces of nature combined to create it. The US National Park Service (NPS) uses the playful acronym DUDE to explain these processes. DUDE stands for deposition, uplift, downcutting, and erosion.

Around two billion years ago, igneous and metamorphic rocks formed in the area. These hard rocks are created by heat and pressure. At times, a shallow ocean covered the region. At other times, the ocean receded and the area was covered in sand dunes. Because of this, hundreds of millions of years of sediment deposits are

Visitors who are interested in geology can see photographs, 3D rock models, and diagrams at Yavapai Geology Museum. It is located at Grand Canyon National Park's Yavapai Point.

▲ At Yavapai Geology Museum, guests can look at the canyon through panoramic windows. Plaques below the windows point out notable sights, including the Colorado River and examples of erosion.

visible on the walls of the Grand Canyon. This deposition process happened layer by layer, giving the canyon a striped appearance.

Uplift, Downcutting, and Erosion

Around 75 million years ago, the tectonic plates beneath the area shifted, pushing the land upward. Usually when this happens, a jagged, mountainous peak often forms. But that didn't happen at the Grand Canyon. The land was pushed to a higher elevation, but the land remained flat.

Scientists are unsure exactly why this happened.

The Colorado River began to carve out the canyon about five to six million years ago. The river rushed through the area, carrying boulders and debris with it. It scoured the soft layers of sediment away to create the Grand Canyon's walls.

> " I see the canyon every day and have gone on many trips to areas 90 percent or more of visitors don't see. But I still haven't even seen half of it.[1]
>
> —Sarah Acomb, Grand Canyon park ranger, in a 2017 interview "

Today, the walls of the canyon are still susceptible to the forces of wind, rain, ice, and snow. As the walls erode, the canyon grows wider. It is also deepening, but at a much slower rate. The Colorado River has already carved away the canyon's softer sediment and has started undercutting its harder igneous and metamorphic rocks, vastly slowing down the process.

Water in the Grand Canyon

Today, the Colorado River flows through the Grand Canyon for about 277 miles (446 km).[2] It moves a massive amount of water through the canyon. But many visitors don't realize that there are lots of other streams of water in the Grand Canyon.

Perennial streams are streams that hold water year-round. There are four major perennial streams within

The Great Unconformity

The Grand Canyon's geological history can be seen in the layers of rock that make up its walls. Geologists have determined the age of the rocks through radiometric dating. This involves measuring the amount of certain radioactive elements or materials in a rock. Through this process, geologists have noticed something strange about the Grand Canyon's rock layers. About 1.2 billion years of Earth's history are missing from them. This missing time is called the Great Unconformity. Geologists aren't sure why the time is missing. It could be due to erosion. It could also be due to nondeposition, or a period in which sediment is not deposited.

the Grand Canyon that flow into the Colorado River.[3] These are Kanab Creek, Havasu Creek, the Little Colorado River, and the Paria River.

The canyon also contains intermittent streams, which hold water during only part of the year. It is home to ephemeral streams too. These exist for only a short time after periods of heavy rainfall. Each stream plays a role in shaping the canyon.

More than a Hole

To the untrained eye, the Grand Canyon may look simply like a vast hole in the ground. But it is much more complicated than that. The canyon contains an intricate maze of side canyons, streams, and hidden waterfalls. It is home to pools, magnificent rock formations, and towering peaks. Visitors can see all kinds of geological wonders in and around the site.

No Dinosaur Bones

The Grand Canyon may look like a place where dinosaurs would have roamed long ago. But none ever did. The canyon didn't exist until around five million years ago, and dinosaurs went extinct more than 65 million years ago. Dinosaur fossils won't be found within the layers of rock lining the canyon walls, either. These rocks are much older than the time in which dinosaurs were living. However, the fossils of ancient marine creatures, including crinoids, brachiopods, and sponges, have been found at the canyon.

⚠ **The Grand Canyon's Zoroaster Temple is named after an Iranian prophet. It has an elevation of 7,123 feet (2,171 m).**

The peaks within the Grand Canyon are called temples. Clarence Dutton, a cartographer and geologist, came up with this name in the 1870s. To his eye, the peaks resembled pagodas in Asia. This naming convention continued throughout the early 1900s, with surveyors designating 23 of the Grand Canyon's peaks as temples.[4]

Each temple was named after a different god or goddess. One example is the Shiva Temple, which towers 7,646 feet (2,331 m) in elevation.[5] It gets its name from the Hindu god Shiva. Other peaks are named Thor, Isis, Buddha, Zoroaster, and Apollo. It's easy to forget how

majestic each temple is when looking at them within the Grand Canyon. If any of the temples were plucked from the canyon and placed elsewhere in the United States, their huge scale would be obvious and impressive.

The Shiva Temple Expedition

In 1937, Dr. Harold Elmer Anthony led an expedition to the top of Shiva Temple, one of the Grand Canyon's most prominent buttes. He believed it to be a biological island cut off from the rest of the land for thousands of years. He thought this because of the temple's steep cliffsides and isolated location. He expected to find unique animals living there. Instead, Anthony found common rodents and small mammals. There were also signs of coyotes and deer. The group even found a box of Kodak film on the butte—proof that it wasn't as unexplored as Anthony believed it to be.

Don't Miss It!

The Trail of Time

The Trail of Time is 2.8 miles (4.5 km) of paved trail along the South Rim of the Grand Canyon.[6] The entrance to the trail is near the Yavapai Geology Museum. The trail is the world's largest geoscience exhibit, showcasing the planet's history.

As visitors walk along the trail, they get a view of two billion years of the canyon's history. There are markers on the ground for every 3.2 feet (1 m) of the trail.[7] Each one represents one million years of geological history.

The Trail of Time includes several sights for visitors who are interested in geology. Sample rocks from the canyon are placed along the trail to show their age. Visitors are welcome to touch the boulders, examining their textures and colors. The oldest rock is placed at the end of the trail. At 1.8 billion years old, it is among the oldest rocks in the Grand Canyon.

Informational plaques and markers are placed along the entire trail. There's a lot for guests to see and learn. As they walk along the Trail of Time, visitors can also take in spectacular views of the Grand Canyon.

Geology Up Close

The Grand Canyon's geology can be seen with the naked eye by looking at the canyon walls and seeing the layers of sediment, which feature varying shades of red, brown, pink, and purple. But most visitors don't know exactly what they're looking at. Visitors interested in learning more about the canyon's formation can visit the Yavapai Geology Museum. It has served as a spot for learning about the canyon's geology since 1928.

The museum is located along the canyon's South Rim and is open daily. It has panoramic windows for viewing the canyon, along with informational placards that tell visitors what to look for. Guests can also walk through the museum, examining its numerous exhibits. One is an enormous sculpted relief map that shows the layout of the Grand Canyon.

CHAPTER
THREE

THE SOUTH RIM

Visitors have flocked to the South Rim of the Grand Canyon for more than 100 years. It's the most visited area of Grand Canyon National Park. More than 90 percent of guests visit this section of the park.[1]

The South Rim is open year-round and is easily accessible by train or car. The area has numerous options for dining and lodging. It offers breathtaking views of the Grand Canyon too. Visitors can hike or bike along the South Rim's trails. Or they can visit the area's many overlooks and historical sites. With so much to see and do on the South Rim, it's easy to understand why it's such a popular destination for visitors from across the country and around the globe.

Inside the Grand Canyon Visitor Center at the South Rim, visitors can see a large map of the canyon. They can also check out a souvenir shop and read informative placards along the walls.

Visitor Center

Whether visitors arrive at the South Rim aboard the Grand Canyon Railway or in a car, the Grand Canyon Visitor Center is the perfect place to begin their trip. Here, guests can find all the information they need for a seamless visit. Inside the Visitor Center, which is open daily, visitors can watch two short films.

> ### Traffic Jam
>
> In the summer months, especially during the peak hours of 9:00 a.m. to 5:00 p.m., visitors should expect heavy traffic at the entrance to the South Rim of Grand Canyon National Park.[3] Parking is limited and can be difficult to find. Many visitors try to arrive before or after the park's peak hours. Parking is also available in the nearby town of Tusayan, located seven miles (11 km) away from the park.[4] During the summer, the town offers free shuttle rides to the South Rim's Grand Canyon Visitor Center.

Grand Canyon: A Journey of Wonder is a 24-minute orientation film. It is shown every half hour. The second film is called *We Are Grand Canyon*. This short film introduces viewers to the Grand Canyon's 11 tribal communities. It is shown every hour.[2]

Sometimes visitors arrive at Grand Canyon National Park during hours when the Visitor Center is closed. If this happens, guests can check out the kiosks and signs outside the building, which provide shuttle schedules, hiking information, and more. The Grand Canyon Visitor Center Shuttle Bus Terminal is located here too. It is the main hub for the park's free bus transportation service.

The shuttle bus service has operated at the South Rim for more than 40 years, providing visitors easy access to overlooks, trailheads, and more. Visitors can hop on and off shuttles at various points along the South Rim.

Canyon Adventures Bike Tours & Café is also located at the Visitor Center. It is the only place to rent bicycles inside the park. Wheelchair rentals are also available there. In addition to rentals, Canyon Adventures Bike Tours & Café offers a variety of food, including sandwiches, pastries, and a full espresso bar. Visitors can fuel up their bodies before embarking on their Grand Canyon adventure.

Mather Point

Mather Point is located just a short walk away from the Visitor Center. Its proximity to the Visitor Center and to several of the South Rim's parking lots makes it the most

Stephen Tyng Mather

Conservationist Stephen Tyng Mather was passionate about preserving public lands. In the early 1900s, he moved to Washington, DC, where he became one of the founders of the National Park Service (NPS). He served as the first director of the NPS from 1917 to 1929. Mather Point, Grand Canyon National Park's most visited overlook, is named after him. The path leading to Mather Point features a monument built to honor Mather and his work in protecting national parks.

⚠ **At Mather Point, park guests can see more than 60 miles (97 km) to the west and more than 30 miles (48 km) to the east on a clear day.**

popular viewing point in Grand Canyon National Park. For most park visitors, it's the first place where they have the opportunity to view the canyon.

The panoramic view from Mather Point showcases the Grand Canyon in all its splendor. Towering rock formations take center stage. Deep below, visitors can see the Colorado River at the bottom of the canyon.

Mather Point is impressive at any time of day, but it really shines at sunrise and sunset. As the sun's position changes in the sky, the light changes within the canyon. This highlights the various colors of the canyon's rock layers. Due to Mather Point's accessibility and popularity, it's one of the most crowded spots in the park. To get the best view possible, many visitors arrive there early in the day.

The Rim Trail

Many visitors at Grand Canyon National Park walk along the Rim Trail. Running parallel to the South Rim for 13 miles (21 km), the Rim Trail offers amazing views of the canyon.[5] Most of the trail is flat and paved, so it's an easy hike that is well suited to families with small children. Some parts of the trail are also wheelchair accessible. Visitors can bike on some sections of the trail too.

> "I just like to keep going back to the same place and continue looking at it, because every day the light's different."[6]
>
> —John Blaustein, photographer, on why he's been photographing the Grand Canyon for more than 40 years

Few people hike the entire length of the Rim Trail. Instead, they get on and off shuttle buses that drive along the route. The Rim Trail also connects the major attractions of the South Rim, including the Visitor Center, Grand Canyon Village, various lodging accommodations, restaurants, trail entrances, and Hermits Rest.

Grand Canyon Village

Grand Canyon Village was built around the Grand Canyon Railway in the early 1900s to accommodate visitors. It's been the tourist hub of the South Rim ever since. Today, the village is home to lodgings, restaurants, souvenir stands, and more.

In addition to the Grand Canyon Train Depot, guests can find the famous El Tovar Hotel in Grand Canyon Village. El Tovar opened in 1905. It's the park's finest hotel, built to resemble a Swiss chalet. It offers world-class lodging and dining. Perched right at the edge of the South Rim, the hotel boasts spectacular views of the canyon.

El Tovar was designated a National Historic Landmark in 1987. Many famous people have stayed at the hotel. Some notable customers include US president Theodore

Are Pets Allowed in the Park?

Dogs and cats are allowed at the South Rim of Grand Canyon National Park. However, they are allowed only above the rim. All pets must be leashed. Pets are not allowed on park buses, inside park lodgings, or on hiking trails beneath the rim, although there are exceptions for service animals. If visitors want to board a bus or hike into the canyon for the day, their pets can be kenneled at the Grand Canyon Kennel. Visitors can arrange daytime care or make overnight arrangements. If guests are staying at the Grand Canyon Railway Hotel, which is located in Williams, Arizona, their pets can stay at the Railway Pet Resort.

▲ **El Tovar Hotel was built out of Oregon pine and limestone local to the Grand Canyon area. Today, the hotel has 78 rooms.**

Roosevelt, famed scientist Albert Einstein, and talk show host Oprah Winfrey.

Kolb Studio is also in Grand Canyon Village. It functions as a small museum. Visitors can see antique cameras, old photographs, and exhibits. They can also watch a video of the Kolb brothers rafting down the Colorado River.

Mary Colter's Buildings

Mary Colter was the chief architect and designer for Fred Harvey Company, one of the companies that established the Grand Canyon as a tourist attraction. Although women were generally not permitted to hold such positions in the early 1900s, Colter was an influential architect. She designed eight buildings on the South Rim, all of which are still standing today.[7]

The first was Hopi House, built in 1905. Colter modeled the building after a Hopi pueblo, a type of traditional home made of stone or adobe bricks. For more than 100 years, Hopi House has served as a souvenir shop that offers authentic American Indian arts and crafts.

Hermits Rest is one of Colter's most famous buildings. Built in 1914, the structure was designed to look like an old miner's cabin. It was constructed with materials native to the area. The building now serves as a gift shop where visitors can purchase souvenirs, drinks, and snacks.

Hermits Rest is also where the Rim Trail ends. It marks the beginning of Hermit Trail, a winding route that leads to backcountry hiking paths beneath the rim. Visitors can catch their breath and take a break at Hermits Rest before beginning their trek into the canyon.

Colter's Lookout Studio is another popular spot on the South Rim. Constructed in 1914, this building was designed to resemble the Grand Canyon's jagged, rocky peaks. It sits on the edge of the canyon, offering breathtaking views and brilliant photo opportunities.

Don't Miss It!

Grand Canyon Star Party

Grand Canyon National Park is committed to eliminating light pollution, or the excess of artificial light in outdoor spaces. Light pollution not only makes the stars in the night sky harder to see but also affects animal behavior. Because of the park's efforts to combat light pollution, it offers some of the best stargazing in the world.

For one week in June, Grand Canyon National Park teams up with the Tucson Amateur Astronomy Association to host the Grand Canyon Star Party. This free annual event takes place on multiple days of the week beginning at sunset. Participants use telescopes set up on the South Rim.

They can get close-up views of the moon or check out distant planets in the solar system. Visitors may even spot a shooting star. The Star Party includes nightly constellation talks, in which rangers use laser pointers to teach guests how to find constellations. The South Rim also hosts night-sky photography workshops.

To avoid contributing to light pollution, visitors are asked to use red flashlights instead of white ones. This is because red flashlights don't harm a person's night vision as much as white flashlights do. A red flashlight can be created by coloring a flashlight's lens with a red marker or red nail polish. The lens can also be covered with red cellophane.

Telescopes at Lookout Studio allow visitors to view deep into the canyon. Lucky visitors may spot elk or other wildlife beneath the rim.

The Desert View Watchtower features intricate rock arrangements that are meant to make the tower blend in with its surroundings. Colter modeled the building after Ancestral Puebloan architecture.

Many people consider Colter's masterpiece to be the Desert View Watchtower. Constructed in 1932, it was designed to blend in with the canyon. It towers more than 70 feet (21 m) above the rim, making it the tallest building on the South Rim.[8]

Guests can go inside the tower for free, but they must get tickets first. From the tower's upper floors, guests can enjoy a thrilling view of the canyon below. The Desert View Watchtower also provides guests with a unique perspective of the Colorado River snaking along the canyon floor.

CHAPTER
FOUR

MAGNIFICENT VIEWS

Most of the Grand Canyon's visitors enjoy simply seeing the canyon with their own eyes. They may spend only a few hours at the park, marveling at the beauty of the red rocks. People looking for these kinds of magnificent vistas can find several easily accessible viewing points along the South Rim.

Each scenic overlook showcases a different view of the canyon. Some give visitors a view of the Colorado River. Others provide a closer look at unique rock features within the canyon.

Desert View Drive

Desert View Drive is a scenic drive located on the South Rim. This 25-mile (40 km) stretch of road begins east of Grand

At many scenic overlooks along Desert View Drive, visitors can read informative plaques that share facts about the area's geology, history, and more.

Canyon Village and ends at the Desert View Watchtower. The road is designed for visitors who are driving their own vehicles, and it includes six canyon viewpoints and four picnic areas. There are also five unmarked pullout locations along Desert View Drive.[1]

> "As the sun comes up and the sun goes down, the colors, shadows, and light will shift continuously, revealing the canyon in many moods.[2]
> —Eric Lindberg, award-winning photographer, on photographing the Grand Canyon

The Grand Canyon's shuttle service does not travel along most of this scenic road, so visitors who don't have their own vehicles must purchase bus tickets. Traveling by bicycle is also an option. Desert View Drive is a high-traffic area with no designated bike lanes, so the conditions aren't ideal for cyclists.

Car Trouble?

People traveling to the Grand Canyon by car should remember that the canyon is not located near a big city. If visitors have issues with their cars, help may not arrive quickly. This means it's important for visitors to make sure their vehicles are well maintained and in good operating condition. Drivers should keep a spare tire and jumper cables in their cars. They should also bring water, snacks, and blankets in case their car breaks down. Park visitors can check road and weather conditions on the Arizona Emergency Information Network's website.

MAGNIFICENT VIEWS   41

For visitors driving along Desert View Drive, the Pipe Creek Vista pullout offers the first view of the Grand Canyon. Because it is the first viewing area, this spot is extremely popular. There are parking spaces and picnic areas available at Pipe Creek Vista, but the site can get crowded during peak hours. Pipe Creek Vista is the only spot along Desert View Drive that is accessible by shuttle. It also includes an entrance to the Rim Trail.

As visitors take in the view from Pipe Creek Vista, they can see the canyon's colorful rocks. They can also spot a forest of evergreen trees in the shade of the canyon walls. The pullout is a popular spot for bird-watchers during the

From Pipe Creek Vista, visitors can spot several temples and buttes. They can also see Pipe Creek, which is part of the Colorado River.

spring and fall bird migrations. During this time, visitors can spot songbirds, hawks, and other species. Some parts of Pipe Creek Vista do not have guardrails, so guests should exercise caution while visiting.

Grandview Point is another popular overlook along Desert View Drive. At approximately 7,400 feet (2,250 m) above sea level, Grandview Point is one of the South Rim's highest points.[3] From this spot, visitors can look to the northeast to see a group of buttes, including Krishna Shrine, Vishnu Temple, Rama Shrine, and Sheba Temple. They can see part of the Colorado River too.

Grandview Point is located directly above the remnants of the Last Chance Mine, where people mined for copper ore between 1893 and 1907. The old mining camp is now listed on the National Register of Historic Places, and visitors can access it via the Grandview Trail.

This trail was once used by mules carrying hundreds of pounds of copper on their backs. They transported it from the mine to the rim. The Grandview Trail is very steep and treacherous, so only experienced hikers who enjoy a challenge should attempt hiking it.

To see the Grand Canyon from the South Rim's highest point, visitors must stop at Navajo Point. Located 7,461 feet (2,274 m) above sea level, this spot offers a

MAGNIFICENT VIEWS

breathtaking view of the canyon, especially at sunrise and sunset.[4] Visitors can see the Colorado River from Navajo Point. They can also see the Desert View Watchtower rising from the rocks.

The Grand Canyon Supergroup

Another popular spot along Desert View Drive is Lipan Point. Located at the canyon's widest point, this overlook offers spectacular panoramic views. Visitors can look out over forests, making the area an excellent spot for bird-watching. They can see the Colorado River from Lipan Point too. The rush of water in Hance Rapid can often be heard at Lipan Point. Here, the Colorado River drops 30 feet (9 m) over the length of the rapids, which is the river's biggest drop within the canyon.[5]

Visit the Park for Free!

To visit Grand Canyon National Park, visitors must purchase a pass. In 2024, the cost of a pass ranged from $20 for single visitors entering by bicycle, by bus, or on foot to $35 per car for visitors entering in a personal vehicle.[6] But on certain days of the year, visitors can enter the park for free. These dates include January 15, which is the birthday of Martin Luther King Jr., and June 19, which is Juneteenth National Independence Day. Admission is also free on the first day of National Park Week, which takes place in April. Other free admission dates are August 4, which is the anniversary of the Great American Outdoors Act; September 28, which is National Public Lands Day; and November 11, which is Veterans Day.

⚠️ **Lipan Point is one of only a few places where park guests can get a clear view of the Grand Canyon Supergroup. They can also spot the Unkar Delta, where Ancestral Puebloan peoples once farmed.**

At Lipan Point, guests can also see parts of the Grand Canyon's geological history. The overlook gives visitors a view of the tilted layers of rocks known as the Grand Canyon Supergroup. These are among the oldest rocks in the canyon. They include reddish igneous and sedimentary rocks, such as sandstone and mudstone. The lower half of the supergroup dates back more than one billion years.

Visitors can also view the Grand Canyon Supergroup from Moran Point, another pullout along Desert View Drive. This point was named after Thomas Moran, a famous landscape artist who first visited the Grand Canyon in 1873. He made a painting of the Grand Canyon titled *The Chasm of the Colorado*. In 1874, Congress purchased it for $10,000.[7] This is equal to about $275,013 in 2024.[8] The painting was placed in the US Capitol. Today, it is displayed at the Smithsonian American Art Museum in Washington, DC.

Secret Spots

There are many popular viewpoints along Desert View Drive, but visitors can also enjoy stunning views at lesser-known spots. One is Yaki Point. This spot isn't accessible by private vehicles, so it's less crowded than other viewpoints along the road. Guests who want to visit Yaki Point can get there by taking the Grand Canyon's free shuttle service. Yaki Point offers great views of the canyon, especially at sunrise and sunset. Visitors can also spot the Desert View Watchtower in the distance.

Capturing the Perfect Photo

Many visitors say that the hours just after sunrise and just before sunset offer the best lighting for photographs of the Grand Canyon. Wide-angle photographs allow people to capture sweeping panoramic views of the park. But to get unique pictures, photographers should also consider zooming in on interesting rock formations. To highlight the magnitude and size of the canyon, photographers can include a person in the picture for scale. Photographers at Grand Canyon National Park should always be mindful of their surroundings, especially when taking photographs in an area with steep cliffs or loose rocks.

Shoshone Point is considered one of the Grand Canyon's best-kept secrets. There's an unmarked pullout with a parking lot on the side of Desert View Drive. After parking, visitors can walk through the forest along a dirt path to reach Shoshone Point. The viewing area includes grills, trash cans, outhouses, and a covered shelter that can be reserved for family reunions or parties. There is no electricity or water at the site.

Shoshone Point features a unique rock formation and amazing overlooks into the canyon. There are no guardrails, so visitors should avoid getting too close to the ledge, especially if there is snow or ice. The dirt trail through the forest can get very muddy after periods of rainfall, so guests should keep that in mind when visiting.

Hermit Road

Another scenic route at Grand Canyon National Park is Hermit Road. To the west of Grand Canyon Village, Hermit Road stretches along the South Rim for seven miles (11 km), offering some of the park's best viewpoints.[9] The road is closed to private vehicles from March to November. During those months, it's accessible by shuttle. Visitors can also book commercial bus tours along the route. Since private vehicles aren't permitted on Hermit Road

⚠️ **Many people consider Trailview Overlook the best spot for getting a bird's-eye view of the Bright Angel Trail switchbacks.**

during most of the year, many visitors explore it on foot or by bicycle.

Trailview Overlook is the first viewpoint along Hermit Road. Stairs lead to viewing stations. The overlook gives visitors a unique view of Bright Angel Trail, a hiking trail with a zigzagging descent. Observers can watch hikers and people riding mules as they travel down into the canyon. From Trailview Overlook, visitors can also spot Grand Canyon Village and the El Tovar Hotel. Bright Angel Creek, a stream that flows into the Colorado River, can be seen from the overlook too.

⚠ **The Powell Memorial at Powell Point is the largest monument in Grand Canyon National Park. The plaque at the top of the memorial lists the names of Powell and the men who were part of his expeditions.**

Another popular spot along Hermit Road is the Abyss. This spot features a sheer drop-off of more than 3,000 feet (914 m).[10] At this location, the canyon wall isn't shaped by the effects of water. Instead, gravity shapes the wall. The constant pull of gravity on the wall causes pieces of rock to fall off over time. White rocks lie scattered across the red slopes of the canyon below the Abyss. These rocks plummeted to the canyon floor during rock falls caused by the force of gravity.

Pima Point is another stop along Hermit Road. It is considered the best spot along the South Rim to hear the Colorado River rushing through the canyon. Sometimes guests can hear the roar of the river's Granite Rapid from Pima Point. For the best chances of hearing the rushing river, guests should visit in the offseason. During this time, there's less noise from crowds of people.

Powell Point is also located on Hermit Road. This viewpoint offers breathtaking views and is home to the Powell Memorial. History buffs can climb a set of stairs to view a large plaque that commemorates Major John Wesley Powell and his crew. Powell led expeditions down the Colorado River into the Grand Canyon. The first was in 1869, and the second was from 1871 to 1872. At a time when little was known about the Grand Canyon, Powell's expeditions helped put it on the map.

Sunset Views

Many visitors believe that Hopi Point, which is located on Hermit Road, is the best place to view the sunset in the Grand Canyon. This is because Hopi Point extends farther into the canyon than other viewpoints in the park, giving visitors an unobstructed panoramic view. As the sun sets, light and shadows change the appearance of the canyon's rock layers. From Hopi Point, visitors can see Shiva Temple to the north. The Colorado River is clearly visible too. Due to Hopi Point's elevation of 7,071 feet (2,155 m), the river appears small. But this segment of the river is actually around 350 feet (107 m) wide, which is almost the length of a football field.[11]

To get a good viewing spot at Hopi Point, visitors should arrive well before sunset during peak months. Those who wish to avoid the crowds may want to visit Hopi Point in late winter or spring. Private vehicles are permitted on Hermit Road in December, January, and February, but park guests should check the local weather conditions before planning a visit. There may be snow and ice during these months.

For most of the year, visitors can access Hopi Point only by taking a shuttle bus. Much of the main overlook area is surrounded by guardrails.

CHAPTER
FIVE

INTO THE CANYON

Whether visitors spend one day or a few weeks at Grand Canyon National Park, they have numerous opportunities to venture below the canyon's rim. For adventurous travelers, descending into the Grand Canyon offers a closer look at the geological forces at work in the area. Anyone planning to enter the canyon should bring good hiking shoes, sunscreen, and plenty of food and water.

It's also wise for hikers to carry a safety whistle or signal mirror. They can use these tools if they get lost. Before hiking, visitors can check the park's notice boards or website for any special alerts.

Hikers at Grand Canyon National Park should be careful not to overestimate their abilities. The NPS warns that "there

While Bright Angel Trail is well maintained, the steep dirt path contains many switchbacks. Hikers must be aware of the sheer drop-offs on the trail's sides.

are no easy trails into or out of the Grand Canyon."[1] It also says that "everyone who hikes in the canyon for the first time reports that it was more difficult than they expected."[2] Most experienced hikers are used to mountainous terrain, with the most strenuous part of the hike being the climb up the trail. The beginning of a hike is usually the most difficult part, so hikers don't need to reserve as much energy for the hike back down.

But for hikes at the Grand Canyon, it is the opposite. The canyon is like an upside-down mountain. Many hikers find themselves in trouble after hiking into the canyon until they're tired. They realize that they haven't reserved enough energy for the climb back to the rim. On average, the climb back up takes twice as long as the hike down into the canyon.[3]

The NPS strongly advises against attempting to hike all the way to the bottom of the canyon and back to the

Share the Trail

In Grand Canyon National Park, hikers and mule riders must share trails. In the canyon, the mules have the right of way. When hikers cross paths with mule riders, the hikers should step out of the way, moving to the uphill side of the trail away from the edge. If a hiker crosses paths with mules, there's no need to panic. The mules in Grand Canyon National Park are highly trained. Hikers should remain calm, stand still, and be quiet until the last mule is 50 feet (15 m) away.[4]

rim in one day. This is not only too physically taxing for most hikers but also doesn't give them enough time to experience the canyon's beauty. Fortunately, Grand Canyon National Park offers plenty of trails for day hikers and visitors of all skill levels.

Bright Angel Trail

Bright Angel Trail is the most popular hiking trail below the canyon rim. This well-maintained path accommodates hikers and mules. While the climb down the trail is deceptively easy, the steep hike back to the rim can be grueling, especially in the hot summer months. The trek to the canyon floor is 9.5 miles (15 km) long.[5] But there are numerous stops along the way, giving hikers the opportunity to plan round-trip day hikes that suit their needs.

For hikers interested in a quick jaunt into the canyon, the First Tunnel along Bright Angel Trail is the perfect choice. This is a short hike to a natural rock tunnel. Just after passing through the tunnel, visitors can stop to see an overhanging rock to their left. The rock has a pictograph panel on it that was painted by American Indians around 4,000 years ago. The painting features antlered deer and other symbols. Experts aren't sure who

▲ **The Three-Mile Resthouse on Bright Angel Trail includes toilets, a water station, and a small stone shelter.**

created these images but note that they resemble other rock art created by Archaic Period peoples.

Two rest houses located on Bright Angel Trail are popular destinations for day hikers. The first is the Mile-and-a-Half Resthouse, located 1,100 feet (335 m) below the rim. This three-mile (4.8 km) round-trip journey is ideal for visitors who want to spend just a few hours in the canyon.[6]

The rest house offers hikers a break from the elements. It includes bathroom facilities and a phone to use in case of emergencies. In the summer, there is also a water-filling station available at the rest house. Another rest house, located about three miles (4.8 km) along Bright Angel Trail, offers a challenging six-mile (9.7 km) round-trip hike.[7]

The Havasupai Gardens are located near the halfway point of Bright Angel Trail. The NPS recommends consulting with a park ranger before attempting a day hike to the Havasupai Gardens. It's a challenging nine-mile (14 km) round-trip hike with a change in elevation of more than 3,000 feet (914 m).[8]

Hikers who make the trip are rewarded with a lush green oasis that features water and shade trees. The Havasupai people farmed in this part of the canyon thousands of years before Grand Canyon National Park was established. Today, the Gardens are home to a basic campground, along with picnic areas, restrooms, and a ranger's station.

No Bikes below the Rim

Visitors can use traditional bicycles and electric bicycles only in certain areas of Grand Canyon National Park. Riding bikes on trails beneath the rim is strictly prohibited. However, there are many areas where bicycle use is permitted and even encouraged. Along the South Rim, there are several miles of roads and Greenway Trails for cyclists to use. Greenway Trails are paved pathways designed for cyclists and pedestrians. Grand Canyon National Park's free shuttle service is also bike friendly. Visitors who grow tired of biking can board a shuttle at any of its designated stops and load their bikes onto the shuttle's bike rack. At the North Rim, mountain bikers can explore the forest on biking trails.

South Kaibab Trail

Another popular path at Grand Canyon National Park is the South Kaibab Trail. This dirt trail leads from the South Rim to the bottom of the canyon. Visitors can hike the entire trail or complete shorter day hikes along the route.

While South Kaibab Trail is maintained by the NPS, it is steeper and more difficult to traverse than Bright Angel Trail. It offers very little shade and has no water stations, so visitors may want to avoid hiking the trail during midday when the sun is directly overhead. But South Kaibab Trail features expansive views of the canyon, and many hikers find it to be the most rewarding hike that Grand Canyon National Park has to offer.

The South Kaibab Trail carves its way down to the Colorado River more quickly than other trails within the park. It begins with a section of steep switchbacks known as the chimney. As hikers descend the chimney, they quickly move through millions of years of Earth's geological history.

Ooh Aah Point is a popular overlook located about one mile

> "The South Kaibab Trail is my favorite trail at the Grand Canyon! It descends quickly (making it a beast to come back up), but the views from this trail are phenomenal."[9]
>
> —Ash Nudd, blogger, podcaster, and former park ranger

⚠ **Hikers on the South Kaibab Trail should prepare for rocky trail conditions. The path also includes narrow switchbacks and steep stairs.**

(1.6 km) from the trailhead of South Kaibab Trail.[10] At this spot, the path opens up into a breathtaking view of the eastern canyon, eliciting exclamations of "Ooh! Aah!" from many visitors. People often turn around at Ooh Aah Point and hike back to the trailhead. Others choose to continue down the trail to Cedar Ridge.

Located farther down South Kaibab Trail, Cedar Ridge has outhouses that visitors can use. But there is no shelter or water there. The NPS does not recommend that anyone attempt to hike farther than Cedar Ridge for a day hike in the summer. Despite being only a three-mile (4.8 km) round trip, the hike to Cedar Ridge has an elevation change of 1,120 feet (341 m), and the climb back to the rim is steep and difficult.[11] Due to the area's desert temperatures and the lack of shade along the trail, hikers can quickly become overheated and susceptible to heatstroke.

During cooler months, experienced hikers may plan day hikes to Skeleton Point, although the NPS recommends consulting a park ranger first. It's six miles (9.7 km) to the overlook and back, with a change in elevation of more than 2,000 feet (610 m).[12] To reach Skeleton Point, hikers continue along South Kaibab Trail. Along the way, they enjoy views of the canyon and O'Neill Butte, one of the park's most recognizable rock structures. When hikers reach Skeleton Point, they're rewarded with an amazing view of the Colorado River.

Hermit Trail

Hermit Trail is more challenging than Bright Angel Trail and South Kaibab Trail. The trail is not maintained by the NPS, so it is rocky and rough. The route's upper section is incredibly steep, with a vertical descent of 2,000 feet (610 m) in 2.5 miles (4 km).[13] Few people attempt to hike

Hermit Trail, and no mules travel along the path, either. But for hikers with the experience and strength for the journey, Hermit Trail is a rewarding hike. It's a great option for people who want to avoid crowds at the park. Hikers may also spot wildlife such as elk and bighorn sheep along the trail.

There are several natural water sources along Hermit Trail. These include the Santa Maria Spring, Hermit Creek, and the Colorado River. Before beginning a hike on Hermit Trail, visitors should check in with a park ranger to see if water is flowing in the spring and the creek. This way, they will know if natural water sources will be available on their hike.

But hikers shouldn't drink directly from these streams. Instead, they should use water purification tablets. These allow hikers to purify the water before drinking it.

> ## Camping in the Grand Canyon
>
> There are several campgrounds within Grand Canyon National Park. These are located along the South Rim and North Rim. However, some adventurous visitors may wish to spend one or several nights beneath the rim. To do so, they must obtain a special backcountry permit. Only a limited number of these permits are awarded each month. To increase their chances of obtaining a permit, visitors can enter a lottery. The lottery winner is granted early access to reserve a camp area. In 2024, the cost to enter the lottery was $10, and the fee was nonrefundable.[14] To learn more about backcountry permits, guests can go to the park's website or visit the park's permits office.

Riding a Mule

Many park visitors choose to explore the Grand Canyon on the back of a mule. Stronger and more sure-footed than horses, mules have been used in the Grand Canyon since the earliest days of tourism in the area. An entrepreneur named John Hance began advertising mule rides into the canyon as early as 1887.

 Mule tours at the South Rim are available to visitors ages nine and up. Participants must wear wide-brimmed hats, long-sleeved shirts, pants, and closed-toe shoes.

On the South Rim, mule tours are offered year-round. Visitors can ride the animals all the way down to the Colorado River. However, reservations for mule tours fill up quickly, often more than a year in advance. It's also important to note that there are certain requirements for riding mules in the Grand Canyon. For example, there are strict requirements for a rider's weight, depending on the duration and difficulty of the trip.

There are height and age requirements too. While riding a mule into the canyon might seem more relaxing than hiking, it can be physically taxing. Riders often have sore muscles at the end of the day. But riding mules is a unique experience that many park visitors enjoy.

On the Colorado River

Adventurous visitors at Grand Canyon National Park have the chance to brave the rapids of the Colorado River. While there are calm stretches of the river within the Grand Canyon, there are also 160 sets of rapids.[15] Most rivers in the United States have rapids that are rated on a system of I to V. But the Grand Canyon's rapids have such unique, complex features that they require their own rating system, ranging in difficulty from 1 to 10. Touring or boating on the Colorado River is not for the faint

⚠ **Several companies offer guided white water rafting tours on the Colorado River. Tours may include camping, sightseeing, and other activities.**

of heart. But being on the river offers an entirely different perspective of the Grand Canyon. Because of this, experiences on the river attract more than 22,000 park visitors each year.[16]

River tours vary in length. A variety of watercraft are available, including motorized rafts, oar-powered rafts, paddle rafts, kayaks, and wooden dories. Visitors can

take guided trips or private, self-guided trips. For private trips, visitors must obtain a permit. The NPS grants a limited number of watercraft permits each year in order to protect the environment and avoid overcrowding. Due to the limited number of watercraft permits granted by the NPS, river tours must be booked about one to two years in advance.[17]

CHAPTER
SIX

THE NORTH RIM

T he North Rim of Grand Canyon National Park receives fewer visitors than the South Rim. On a map, only ten miles (16 km) separate the two rims. But the driving distance from the South Rim to the North Rim is more than 210 miles (338 km). It's a long journey, and only 10 percent of the park's guests visit the North Rim.[1] This makes the area perfect for guests who prefer a more relaxed visit.

Due to its average elevation of 8,000 feet (2,438 m)—more than 1,000 feet (305 m) higher in elevation than the South Rim—the North Rim boasts some of the best views in Grand Canyon National Park.[2] Its forested land and meadows also offer some of the park's best wildlife viewing opportunities. The North Rim is

The North Rim is known for its peaceful atmosphere and sweeping views of the canyon. Cape Royal, *pictured*, is the North Rim's southernmost overlook spot.

home to many species of mammals, including mule deer, elk, and bison.

However, the North Rim's higher elevation means that its temperature is much cooler than the South Rim. The area experiences significant snowfall in the fall, winter, and spring. Because of this, most of the North Rim is closed every year from October 16 through May 14. This includes the North Rim Visitor Center, the North Rim Campground, and Grand Canyon Lodge. Day passes to the North Rim are issued from October 16 through November 30 unless weather conditions force road closures earlier. All roads to the North Rim are closed from December 1 to May 14, unless access roads are closed sooner due to snow.

Grand Canyon Lodge

Grand Canyon Lodge is the hub of the North Rim.

A Big Problem

The American bison is the largest mammal in North America, with adult males weighing thousands of pounds. The North Rim of Grand Canyon National Park is home to the Kaibab Plateau Bison Herd. Because of a lack of natural predators and because hunting is prohibited within the park, the herd grew to include nearly 600 animals by 2017.[3] These large numbers of bison began causing major problems. They trampled vegetation, threatened archaeological sites, and even posed a danger to park guests. Since 2018, state, federal, and tribal agencies have worked together to reduce the number of bison at the North Rim, relocating more than 300 animals.[4]

⚠ **Grand Canyon Lodge features a large terrace that looks out over the canyon. Visitors can relax in chairs or sit at tables while enjoying the view.**

Open from May 15 through October 15, it is the only place on the North Rim that offers lodging, dining options, and shopping. Since it's the only hotel in the area, visitors must book reservations for a room or for one of the nearby cabins well in advance.

The original lodge was built in 1928 but was destroyed in a fire a few years later. The current lodge was completed in 1937 and is listed on the National Register of Historic Places. Built with ponderosa pine beams and featuring a gigantic limestone facade, Grand Canyon Lodge is known for its rustic style.

Arizona State Route 67 is the main access road to the North Rim. The road ends at Grand Canyon Lodge, meaning the hotel is the first thing visitors see when they arrive. From here, there's no view of the canyon—but that's on purpose. The architect of Grand Canyon Lodge, Gilbert Stanley Underwood, wanted to provide guests with a surprise view from inside the lodge. Nearly 100 years later, hotel guests get the same experience.

After walking through the lodge and down the stairs to the sunroom, visitors get their first view of the canyon from the North Rim through the room's large windows. All park guests are welcome to stroll through the lodge or visit its patio to enjoy the view, even if they aren't staying at the lodge. Visitors can also check out the restaurants, post office, and gift shop located in the hotel.

In the lobby of Grand Canyon Lodge, guests can see a life-size statue of a donkey known as Brighty the Burro. It was built in 1966 to honor a real donkey named Brighty, who captured the hearts of Grand Canyon visitors in the early 1900s. For good luck, guests often rub the statue's nose. Today, Brighty's nose gleams from the many years of loving pets it has received from North Rim visitors.

Dining at the North Rim

Dining options are limited at the North Rim. The Grand Canyon Lodge Dining Room is the go-to spot for fine dining in the area. Located inside the lodge, this restaurant features high ceilings, rustic stone walls, and breathtaking views of the canyon. The southwestern steak house serves beef, venison, and bison. It also offers fish and vegetarian dishes. To eat at the Grand Canyon Lodge Dining Room, visitors must make reservations in advance.

Another dining option in the North Rim is Roughrider Saloon, which is also located at Grand Canyon Lodge. This restaurant serves coffee, pastries, and breakfast burritos in the morning. It offers snacks and beverages later in the day. For an affordable meal, visitors can choose to eat at Deli in the Pines. Located next to the lodge, this deli offers sandwiches, salads, and pizza.

Bird-Watching in the Grand Canyon

More than 450 species of birds can be found within Grand Canyon National Park.[5] Among them are several threatened and endangered bird species. One is the Mexican spotted owl, which nests within the inner canyon. The endangered Yuma clapper rail makes its home near the canyon's streams and rivers. Lucky visitors may even spot a California condor, one of the world's most endangered species, flying high above the canyon floor. The largest bird in North America, condors are known for having very long wingspans.

Off the Beaten Path

The Rainbow Rim Trail

Visitors looking for a unique experience in Grand Canyon National Park can try mountain biking on the Rainbow Rim Trail. Located along the North Rim, this trail offers the perfect mountain-biking experience. It is about 28 miles (45 km) one way and connects five scenic overlooks, all of which offer stunning views of the Grand Canyon.[6]

The trail leads bikers through a ponderosa pine forest, past meadows, and through steep-sided canyon walls. The forest opens into each overlook, providing sweeping panoramic views of the canyon. Bikers can also spot prominent rock features such as the Powell Plateau.

Motorized vehicles, including e-bikes, are not allowed on the Rainbow Rim Trail. However, mountain bikers may occasionally cross paths with hikers or horseback riders. Bikers often see an abundance of wildlife on the trail, spotting animals such as mule deer, elk, and turkeys. Mountain lions are sometimes seen in the area too. Bikers should keep their distance from all wild animals they see on the Rainbow Rim Trail.

Before beginning their bike ride, visitors should note that this part of the North Rim is remote. Cell phone service is limited. Bikers may want to bring a satellite phone or safety whistle along for their journey.

Scenic Drives

Visitors driving to the North Rim along Arizona State Route 67 enjoy breathtaking views on their way to the park. They drive through the Kaibab National Forest, passing lakes, streams, and flowering meadows that teem with wildlife such as deer and turkeys. Before reaching the North Rim entrance, drivers can choose to explore several unpaved forest service roads. These roads can be difficult for drivers to navigate depending on the weather conditions. But visitors who take these paths can access spots such as Crazy Jug Point, which offers an amazing view of the canyon and the Colorado River.

The North Rim's scenic drive is called Cape Royal Road, and it leads to several must-see spots, including hiking trails, overlooks, and even an ancient American Indian site. The road is closed from December 1 through May 14 due to heavy snowfall and wintry conditions. It is often temporarily closed in the fall due to winter storms or fallen trees, so visitors should be sure to check the road conditions before arriving. Cape Royal Road is narrow, winding, and unsafe when covered in snow and ice, so visitors should also keep an eye on weather conditions.

One notable spot along Cape Royal Road is Point Imperial. It is the highest point on either side of the canyon, with an elevation of 8,803 feet (2,683 m).[7] From Point Imperial, visitors can see where the steep, narrow walls of Marble Canyon open into the Grand Canyon. The spot also offers spectacular views of the Painted Desert to the east, the Vermillion Cliffs to the north, and Utah's Navajo Mountain.

    Another pullout along Cape Royal Road is the Walhalla Glades Pueblo. Here, visitors can see the remains of an

Angels Window is located near the end of Cape Royal Road. Visitors can hike over the arch to reach a fenced scenic overlook.

ancient American Indian site. The Ancestral Puebloan peoples lived above and below the rim of the Grand Canyon around 1,000 years ago.

Park guests can tour the site and see the ruins of an Ancestral Puebloan dwelling. History buffs can read signs along the trail that provide information about the American Indian peoples who once lived in the canyon. Guests should behave respectfully at the site and be careful not to damage any ruins.

One of the most popular overlooks along Cape Royal Road is Cape Royal. The trail to this overlook is level and paved, making it easily accessible for park guests. From Cape Royal, visitors can see Angels Window, a natural stone arch that forms the top of a giant hole in the rock. This rock feature gives visitors a unique photography opportunity from the North Rim.

> "There will never be a photograph of the Grand Canyon that can adequately describe its depth, breadth and true beauty.[8]
>
> —*Stefanie Payne, author of* A Year in the National Parks: The Greatest American Road Trip"

Cape Royal provides panoramic views of the Grand Canyon too. As guests gaze across the canyon, they can see the Desert View Watchtower rising above the South Rim. The views from Cape Royal are particularly beautiful at sunrise and sunset.

Take a Hike

The North Rim is home to some of the best hiking trails in Grand Canyon National Park, including trails that explore the alpine forest. At the North Rim, the forest often extends right to the canyon's edge, so hikers should always be mindful of their surroundings. To stay safe, visitors should follow only marked trails.

Bright Angel Point Trail is a short hike that begins at Grand Canyon Lodge. This makes the route a convenient option for North Rim visitors. As the trail nears the canyon's edge, observant hikers will notice the transition from lush, green ponderosa pines to a stunted forest of juniper trees. What stands out most to many hikers are the stunning views along the narrow path. However, hikers on Bright Angel Point Trail should avoid getting distracted because there are spots where the path drops off steeply on both sides.

Mule Rides

For park visitors who want to ride a mule into the Grand Canyon, it's much easier to book a ride at the North Rim than it is at the South Rim. In fact, eager riders can make reservations in the lobby of Grand Canyon Lodge. However, there are no mule rides offered at the North Rim that carry riders all the way down to the Colorado River. North Rim mule rides can range in length. Mule rides are not available when the North Rim is closed from October 16 through May 14.

▲ **Some visitors on the North Kaibab Trail hike to the Redwall Bridge, which is a 5.2-mile (8.4 km) round-trip hike.**

The North Kaibab Trail is the only maintained trail that leads from the North Rim to the bottom of the canyon. It is considered one of the most challenging hikes in Grand Canyon National Park. As a result, it's also the least visited trail. For experienced hikers who are up for the challenge, this makes North Kaibab Trail an excellent choice for descending into the canyon.

For part of the way, hikers must share the trail with mules. As is the case for trails on the South Rim, which are easier and lower in elevation, guests should not attempt to hike from the North Rim to the bottom of the canyon and back in one day. For day-trippers, there are numerous stopping points along the North Kaibab Trail that offer strenuous hikes with canyon views. One is Coconino Overlook, which offers a 1.4-mile (2.3 km) round-trip hike.[9]

CHAPTER
SEVEN

THE PEOPLE OF THE GRAND CANYON

Certain sections of the Grand Canyon are not part of Grand Canyon National Park. These areas of land are located on American Indian reservations. There are 11 American Indian tribes associated with the Grand Canyon.[1] Today, only the Hualapai, meaning "People of the Tall Pines," and the Havasupai, meaning "People of the Blue-Green Water," still own part of their original territory in the Grand Canyon.

Both the Hualapai and the Havasupai have opened their lands to tourists on their own terms. Since they are sovereign American Indian nations, these tribes' areas of the canyon are not governed by the NPS, and they do not have to adhere to the same restrictions. For example, commercial helicopter tours are not permitted within

In 2024, Havasupai leaders Matthew Putesoy, *left*, and Thaddeus Wecogame, *right*, performed with traditional instruments at the Havasupai Indian Reservation.

the national park but are available on tribal land at the tribe's discretion.

When visiting these parts of the Grand Canyon, guests should remember that the tribes are granting them the privilege of visiting their ancestral lands. The area has been sacred to their people for many centuries. This includes not only the land that the tribes currently own and control but all of the Grand Canyon.

The West Rim

The ancestral homelands of the Hualapai once included more than seven million acres (2.8 million ha) of land both above and below the rim of the Grand Canyon. The Hualapai hunted, farmed land, and traded with other tribes who called the Grand Canyon home. In 1883, the US government forced the Hualapai people to relocate to a designated area, the Hualapai Indian Reservation. The Hualapai were

Helicopter and Pontoon Tour

One unique West Rim excursion offers adventurous visitors the chance to experience the Grand Canyon from both the sky and the river. People can book the Helicopter and Pontoon Tour. During this tour, guests ride in a helicopter, enjoying aerial views of the Grand Canyon below. Then the helicopter descends thousands of feet to the bottom of the canyon. Passengers board a boat and cruise along a peaceful stretch of the Colorado River, admiring close-up views of the canyon walls. After that, the helicopter returns guests to the rim.

able to keep just one million acres (404,700 ha) of their ancestral lands.[2]

The Hualapai Indian Reservation includes what is now known as the West Rim of the Grand Canyon. The Hualapai have made the area into a popular tourist destination, offering exciting attractions such as the Grand Canyon Skywalk glass bridge at Eagle Point. This is located just a few hours away from Las Vegas, Nevada.

The location is convenient and easily accessible, especially for people who want to spend just one day at the canyon. Visitors can book tours and buses that travel between Las Vegas and the West Rim. Many Las Vegas casinos and hotels offer these.

Guests can also get a unique experience of the Grand Canyon by visiting the West Rim's Guano Point. This overlook extends out into the canyon, offering dramatic 360-degree views of the landscape. Visitors can see the remnants of an aerial tramway system that carried miners to Bat Cave Mine from 1957 to 1959. This cave was full of guano, or bat feces. At that time, guano was used for fertilizer and dynamite, making it a valuable material.

However, the cave proved to be a disappointment to its owners, providing far less guano than anticipated. In 1959, a US Air Force pilot who was recklessly flying a jet

Don't Miss It!

The Grand Canyon Skywalk at Eagle Point

The Grand Canyon Skywalk at Eagle Point is one of the West Rim's most famous attractions. This horseshoe-shaped glass bridge extends over the Grand Canyon into open air more than 4,000 feet (1,219 m) above the ground, giving visitors a bird's-eye view of the canyon.[3] With its clear glass bottom, the bridge is not for the faint of heart. Even people who aren't afraid of heights sometimes find it daunting to walk the length of the bridge.

However, there's nothing to fear. The Skywalk is a marvel of modern engineering, built to hold many times more weight than it experiences with crowds of visitors. The Skywalk can also withstand hurricane-force winds and powerful earthquakes.

Visitors must purchase tickets to go on the Skywalk at Eagle Point. Before visiting, guests should know that personal belongings such as purses, cell phones, and cameras are not permitted on the bridge. Belongings can be stored in lockers for no additional charge.

Visitors can't take their own photographs on the Skywalk. But professional photographers are available at the site to take pictures for guests. To walk on the Skywalk, visitors must also cover their shoes with booties to protect the bridge's glass surface.

THE PEOPLE OF THE GRAND CANYON

too low crashed into the tramway. The pilot survived, but the tramway was destroyed.

Guano Point is also an important site for the Hualapai. It is said that many generations ago, Hualapai people leapt to their deaths from Guano Point to avoid being captured by white soldiers. The Hualapai encourage guests to honor these people when visiting Guano Point.

The West Rim gives visitors an opportunity to learn more about the American Indian tribes who lived in and around the Grand Canyon for centuries before

Visitors can climb on the rocks at Guano Point. Many people follow a fenceless trail called Highpoint Hike, which leads to the top of the point.

▲ **Supai Village is home to a church, a post office, a lodge, a museum, and several stores and restaurants.**

Grand Canyon National Park was created. At the Native American Village, which is located at Eagle Point, visitors learn about the culture of the Hualapai people. They can take a self-guided tour through traditional housing and sweat lodges, a type of ceremonial sauna. Guests can also watch Indigenous performances at an outdoor theater and purchase handmade items made by the Hualapai, Hopi, and Mojave tribes.

The Havasupai

The Havasupai are the only American Indians who currently live below the canyon's rim. They reside in Havasu Canyon, which is located within the Grand Canyon.

> " I really want the millions of tourists who come to the Grand Canyon to know that we still live inside the park and we still do our best to protect the area.[4]
>
> —*Ophelia Watahomigie-Corliss, Havasupai councilwoman, in a 2019 interview* "

Anthropologists believe the Havasupai have lived continuously inside the canyon for 800 years. For centuries, the Havasupai people planted crops and orchards, hunted animals, and traveled throughout the Grand Canyon freely. Many trails created by the Havasupai are now used by the NPS.

In 1880, US president Rutherford B. Hayes established the Havasupai Indian Reservation, which was eventually whittled down to just 500 acres (202 ha) at the base of Havasu Canyon. When Grand Canyon National Park was established, it entirely encircled the reservation. In 1975, Congress returned 185,000 acres (74,867 ha) of historical tribal plateau lands to the tribe. Congress also agreed to grant the tribe access to an additional 95,000 acres (38,445 ha) to use for ceremonial practices.[5] Today, the

Fly like an Eagle

For visitors who aren't afraid of heights, the West Rim's Grand Canyon Zip Line offers a thrilling, one-of-a-kind trip over the canyon. From 500 feet (152 m) above the canyon, zip liners fly through the sky like eagles, reaching speeds of almost 40 miles per hour (64 kmh). For safety purposes, zip liners must store all personal belongings in a locker, which is provided at no additional cost. There are also strict requirements regarding the zip liner's weight. To ride the zip line, people must weigh between 90 pounds (41 kg) and 275 pounds (125 kg).[6] They must also attend a safety briefing before going on the zip line.

THE PEOPLE OF THE GRAND CANYON

Mule Train Delivery

The Havasupai Indian Reservation is so remote that cars are unable to drive there. However, the United States Postal Service (USPS) provides mail delivery service to Supai Village. It does so with the help of pack mules. Each day, 10 to 22 mules carry mail to the Havasupai people, guided by a wrangler on horseback. Each mule can carry up to 200 pounds (91 kg) of mail.[8] Boxes are tied to the animal's back, with the weight distributed evenly on both sides of the mule.

Havasupai and the NPS work in cooperation to decide how these additional acres are used.

The Havasupai lands are extremely remote and difficult to access. The Havasupai are committed stewards of the land and issue only a small number of permits to tourists at a time. No one is allowed on the Havasupai Indian Reservation without a permit. Due to its remote location and the tribe's careful consideration when issuing permits, crowds are not a problem in Havasu Canyon.

Visitors who have a permit can take a four-hour drive from the South Rim to Hualapai Hilltop. They must then hike eight miles (13 km) to the lodge and tourist office. Visitors staying at the campground must hike an additional two miles (3.2 km) beyond that.[7] Because this hike is challenging, day hiking is prohibited. Only guests who are staying at the campground can hike the trail.

Guests are required to book reservations for a room at the lodge or a space at the campground. Reservations must be for a minimum of three days and should be made well in advance.[9] For visitors who prefer not to make the arduous hike, helicopter rides to Supai Village—a Havasupai village home to about 200 people—are sometimes available on a first-come-first-served basis.[10] Tribal members receive priority boarding. To access some areas, such as waterfalls, helicopter passengers still need to hike several miles.

The Havasupai Waterfalls

The Havasupai lands are famous for their waterfalls. The mineral water in the Havasupai waterfalls is rich with magnesium, which gives it a bright aqua color. The contrast of the blue-green waters against the red rocks of the canyon walls is striking. During the hike from Hualapai Hilltop to Supai Village, hikers pass three of these waterfalls: Fifty Foot Falls, Lower Navajo Falls, and Havasu Falls.[11] Havasu Falls is the most popular due to its large pools. After a long hike, many visitors enjoy swimming in these pools.

Mooney Falls and Beaver Falls are located beyond the campground. Visitors can take in spectacular views from the top of Mooney Falls. The rocks along the trail often become very slick with the spray of the water, so visitors must watch their step. Beaver Falls, located past the campground, has several swimming holes.

> **Havasu Falls drops more than 100 feet (30.5 m) into a large blue pool. During the spring and summer months, the water in the pool is usually around 60 to 70 degrees Fahrenheit (15.6–21°C).**

CHAPTER
EIGHT

STAYING SAFE

While Grand Canyon National Park offers many spectacular views and once-in-a-lifetime experiences, it can also be a dangerous place. Many visitors have been injured, and some have even died. A few hundred people must be rescued from the canyon every year. According to the Grand Canyon Search and Rescue Team, most distress calls are for "slips, trips and falls combined with fatigue [or] physical condition."[1]

To stay safe while visiting Grand Canyon National Park, visitors should follow the rules, make good choices, and be mindful of their surroundings at all times. Guests should never climb over safety rails. The NPS deliberately chooses where to put rails and barriers in order to keep visitors safe.

Signs at trailheads and along hiking trails in Grand Canyon National Park provide maps, safety reminders, and information about weather conditions. Many signs remind people to "hike smart."

▲ **Park officials frequently post the day's expected high and low temperatures online and on displays throughout Grand Canyon National Park.**

However, falls are not the leading cause of death in Grand Canyon National Park. Heart attacks lead to the greatest number of park fatalities. This means it's incredibly important for guests to be aware of their bodies' limitations. Guests should drink and carry plenty of water during their visit. They should also wear hats for sun protection and take frequent breaks while hiking, especially on trails beneath the rim. Hikers should travel in groups of two or more people when possible. Visitors can also consider booking a guided tour as an extra safety precaution.

Extreme Temperatures

Many visitors are caught off guard by the intense heat below the Grand Canyon's rim. As the elevation drops, the temperature rises. With every 1,000-foot (305 m) drop in elevation, the temperature inside the canyon increases by 5.5 degrees Fahrenheit (3.1°C).[2] At the rim, visitors are basically standing on top of a mountain.

As the sun rises, the low humidity, clear skies, and limited shade within the canyon combine to create extreme temperatures at the bottom. It is not uncommon for temperatures to soar well above 100 degrees Fahrenheit (38°C) in the summer. The hottest temperature recorded in the park was at Phantom Ranch, the only lodging available at the bottom of the canyon, where temperatures have reached 120 degrees Fahrenheit (49°C) on more than one occasion.[3]

Winter weather conditions, particularly on the North Rim, can also pose a danger to park guests. The lowest temperature ever recorded within Grand Canyon National Park was −22 degrees Fahrenheit (−30°C) at the North Rim.[4] If visitors are improperly dressed for this kind of wintry weather, they can be susceptible to cold-related dangers.

Icy road conditions can threaten the safety of park visitors too. Heavy snowfall forces roads to close for several months of the year. This is why the North Rim remains closed during the winter.

Lightning

Lightning is one of the most dangerous weather events at Grand Canyon National Park. Lightning strikes can be deadly. People should always check the weather forecast before visiting the park. If a guest hears thunder, sees a storm approaching, or suddenly feels their hair stand on end while visiting the park, it may mean lightning is about to strike. The guest should move away from the canyon walls, avoid touching metal, and seek shelter immediately.

Flash Floods

Flash floods are another threat in Grand Canyon National Park. They can quickly cause dangerous conditions within the canyon. Between mid-June and mid-September, Arizona's monsoon season can bring heavy rains to the Grand Canyon area.

STAYING SAFE

In September 2024, a flash flood on the Havasupai Indian Reservation caused significant damage, burying everything in several feet of mud. The flooding led to the death of a 33-year-old woman named Chenoa Nickerson. She was from Gilbert, Arizona.

The flash flood also swept Chenoa's husband, Andrew Nickerson, into the water. He was saved by a group of

In 2024, members of the US Army helped people evacuate the Supai Village area after flash flooding occurred in parts of Grand Canyon National Park.

people who were rafting down the river. Later, Andrew posted about the experience on social media. "I was seconds from death when a random stranger jumped from his river raft and risked his life without hesitation to rescue me from the raging waters," he wrote. Three days later, another rafting team discovered Chenoa's body in the river.[5]

> "It's part of our monsoon season . . . that rain comes down and doesn't have anywhere to go, and so it can channel off and cause a lot of harm for folks that are in the way."[6]
> —Erinanne Saffell, climatologist, on the 2024 flash flood in Havasu Canyon

Hikers in Havasu Canyon rushed to get to higher ground during the 2024 flash flood. They watched in horror as the blue-green waters of the Havasupai waterfalls turned brown and swelled until the water swallowed everything up. Some hikers tucked themselves into nooks and crannies in the canyon walls until they could be rescued by helicopter.

To avoid these dangers, guests should always check the weather forecast before visiting Grand Canyon National Park. The park's website regularly posts information about weather conditions and potential flood warnings. The website also provides tips for staying safe and alert while hiking in areas where flash floods may occur. Visitors can learn more about this at the park's visitor centers.

Venomous Snakes

Visitors at Grand Canyon National Park should also keep an eye out for dangerous wildlife in the area, such as snakes. Nine species of venomous rattlesnakes live around the Grand Canyon. Below the rim, four species have been documented.[7] They are the black-tailed rattlesnake, the speckled rattlesnake, the western rattlesnake, and the western diamondback rattlesnake.

A bite from any of these snakes could be serious and potentially fatal, requiring a trip to the hospital for antivenin. Antivenin neutralizes the effects of a snake's venom in the human body. It is effective but very expensive. Rattlesnake bites

---

Gila Monster

Grand Canyon National Park is home to North America's largest lizard, the Gila monster. This venomous lizard can grow very long. The bite of a Gila monster is seldom fatal to humans but can cause side effects such as swelling, intense burning, vomiting, low blood pressure, and an increased heart rate. Gila monsters spend most of their time in hidden burrows, so it is rare for park guests to be bitten by one. If a visitor is bitten, they should remain calm and seek medical attention immediately.

⚠ **Five rattlesnake species found in the Grand Canyon live within the national park's boundaries. These snakes are known for their diamond-shaped heads and rattling tails.**

in the United States are almost never deadly. Only a small percentage of these bites result in death.

While snakebites are a scary prospect, they are rare. Snakes will strike humans in self-defense if necessary, but they prefer to hide or slither away. Visitors at Grand Canyon National Park should admire any snakes they see from a safe distance.

Grand Canyon Park Rangers

The park rangers at the Grand Canyon are the most knowledgeable people in the park. Their goal is to keep visitors safe. Guests should get to know park rangers, listen to their educational talks, and ask them about hiking trails, bus schedules, and weather forecasts.

Park rangers can be found at the visitor centers on both the South and North Rims and at ranger stations within the canyon. Rangers also lead programs at various locations throughout the park. These include the Grand Canyon Village and Desert View Watchtower.

Preventative Search and Rescue Rangers can be found walking along trails in the park too. These rangers engage with park visitors to make sure they're okay, have plenty of water, and haven't embarked on a hike that's too tough for them to manage. Talking to the experts can help guests get the most out of a visit to Grand Canyon National Park, ensuring a fun and safe trip for the whole family.

Most Dangerous Animal

One animal has earned a reputation as Grand Canyon National Park's most dangerous creature. It's not the enormous bison, the antlered elk, or the toothy mountain lion. It's the rock squirrel. This small, furry animal looks adorable but has a nasty bite, injuring more park visitors than any other animal. Some guests are bitten while attempting to take a photograph of a rock squirrel. Many others are bitten while attempting to feed one. While visiting, guests should remember that feeding wildlife in Grand Canyon National Park is strictly prohibited.

ESSENTIAL FACTS

GRAND CANYON NATIONAL PARK BASICS

- The Grand Canyon is a massive canyon in northern Arizona. With layers of red rock exposed by millions of years of erosion, the canyon serves as a time capsule of Earth's past.

- The Grand Canyon is 18 miles (29 km) wide at its widest point and one mile (1.6 km) deep at its deepest point. It stretches 277 miles (446 km) long. The Colorado River runs through it.

- Grand Canyon National Park was established in 1919. Today, more than six million people visit every year.

- The South Rim is the most visited area of Grand Canyon National Park. It is home to many scenic overlooks, hiking trails, and educational buildings.

- Only 10 percent of park guests visit the canyon's North Rim. This area is higher in elevation than the South Rim.

- Some parts of the Grand Canyon are not part of Grand Canyon National Park. These areas belong to the Hualapai and Havasupai peoples.

THINGS TO SEE AND DO

- Stop by the Grand Canyon Visitor Center on the South Rim to chat with park rangers.

- Enjoy the view at Mather Point, the most popular overlook in Grand Canyon National Park.

- Go hiking on Bright Angel Trail, South Kaibab Trail, or Hermit Trail.

- Walk out on the glass-bottomed bridge of the Grand Canyon Skywalk at Eagle Point.

- Drive along scenic Cape Royal Road on the North Rim.

MAP

QUOTE

"The Grand Canyon fills me with awe. It is beyond comparison—beyond description."

—President Theodore Roosevelt, on visiting the Grand Canyon in 1903

GLOSSARY

alpine
Relating to the mountains.

arduous
Difficult and exhausting.

butte
An isolated mountain or hill with a flat top and steep sides.

cartographer
A person who makes maps.

conquistador
A Spanish explorer or soldier who conquers new territory.

conservationist
A person who works to protect natural environments and wildlife.

entrepreneur
A person who starts a new business.

erosion
The process by which land is worn away by water and wind.

expedition
A journey to search for a specific place or site.

geoscience
The study of Earth.

igneous
Describing rocks formed by magma.

Indigenous
Native to a particular place.

metamorphic
Describing rocks formed by heat and pressure.

oasis
A green area in a desert.

pagoda
A tower with many stories, each with its own roof, often built as part of a Buddhist temple.

pictograph
A painting on a rock wall.

prospector
A person who searches for gold, oil, or other valuable materials.

sediment
An accumulation of sand and dirt.

sovereign
Describing a tribal nation or group that has the right to govern itself, its lands, and its people.

tectonic plates
Giant slabs of rock that form Earth's crust.

ADDITIONAL RESOURCES

SELECTED BIBLIOGRAPHY

Bitler, Teresa, et al. *Arizona & the Grand Canyon*. Fodor's Travel, 2024.

"Grand Canyon: Plan Your Visit." *National Park Service*, 30 Nov. 2024, nps.gov. Accessed 19 Nov. 2024.

Yogerst, Joe. "Everything You Need to Know about Grand Canyon National Park." *National Geographic*, 3 Jan. 2025, nationalgeographic.com. Accessed 19 Nov. 2024.

FURTHER READINGS

Lassieur, Allison. *The National Parks Encyclopedia*. Abdo, 2023.

Mills, Andrea. *National Parks*. DK, 2023.

Pitts, Christopher. *Grand Canyon National Park*. Lonely Planet, 2024.

ONLINE RESOURCES

To learn more about Grand Canyon National Park, please visit **abdobooklinks.com** or scan this QR code. These links are routinely monitored and updated to provide the most current information available.

MORE INFORMATION

For more information on this subject, contact or visit the following organizations:

GRAND CANYON CONSERVANCY

P.O. Box 399
Grand Canyon, AZ 86023
grandcanyon.org

The Grand Canyon Conservancy is a nonprofit organization dedicated to protecting the Grand Canyon's natural beauty and cultural heritage. It raises funds, educates the public, and operates retail stores throughout Grand Canyon National Park.

GRAND CANYON VISITOR CENTER (SOUTH RIM)

8 South Entrance Rd.
Grand Canyon Village, AZ 86023
nps.gov/grca/planyourvisit/grand-canyon-visitor-center.htm

The Grand Canyon Visitor Center at the South Rim provides visitors with information about Grand Canyon National Park, including maps, hiking trail information, and schedules. Visitors can watch informational videos, view exhibits, and participate in educational programs at the Visitor Center.

NATIONAL PARK SERVICE (NPS)

1849 C St. NW
Washington, DC 20240
nps.gov

The National Park Service (NPS) is a federal agency that manages national parks in the United States, including Grand Canyon National Park.

SOURCE NOTES

CHAPTER 1. A NATIONAL TREASURE

1. "Grand Canyon: Nature & Science." *National Park Service*, 16 July 2018, nps.gov. Accessed 29 Jan. 2025.
2. "Grand Canyon: Geology." *National Park Service*, 1 Oct. 2024, nps.gov. Accessed 29 Jan. 2025.
3. "Living History Performance of President Theodore Roosevelt." *National Park Service*, 24 Feb. 2015, nps.gov. Accessed 29 Jan. 2025.
4. "Mexican-American War." *Britannica*, 19 Dec. 2024, britannica.com. Accessed 29 Jan. 2025.
5. "Grand Canyon: Explorers." *National Park Service*, 5 Sept. 2024, nps.gov. Accessed 29 Jan. 2025.
6. "Grand Canyon: How Do I Get to the South Rim?" *National Park Service*, 23 Dec. 2024, nps.gov. Accessed 29 Jan. 2025.
7. "Schedule & Route." *Grand Canyon Railway & Hotel*, n.d., thetrain.com. Accessed 29 Jan. 2025.
8. Francine Uenuma. "The Fight to Save the Grand Canyon." *Smithsonian Magazine*, 26 Feb. 2019, smithsonianmag.com. Accessed 29 Jan. 2025.
9. "Address of Roosevelt at Grand Canyon." *Theodore Roosevelt Center*, n.d., theodorerooseveltcenter.org. Accessed 29 Jan. 2025.
10. "The Grand Canyon and the Antiquities Act." *National Park Service*, 11 Aug. 2021, nps.gov. Accessed 29 Jan. 2025.
11. Joe Yogerst. "Grand Canyon National Park." *National Geographic*, 3 Jan. 2025, nationalgeographic.com. Accessed 29 Jan. 2025.

CHAPTER 2. GEOLOGICAL HISTORY

1. Dylan Taylor-Lehman. "I Am a Grand Canyon Park Ranger." *Yellow Springs News*, 10 Feb. 2017, ysnews.com. Accessed 29 Jan. 2025.
2. "Colorado River in the Grand Canyon." *American Rivers*, n.d., americanrivers.org. Accessed 29 Jan. 2025.
3. "Grand Canyon: Rivers and Streams." *National Park Service*, 8 Apr. 2021, nps.gov. Accessed 29 Jan. 2025.
4. Mike Buchheit. "Sacred Temples in a Sacred Place." *Arizona Highways*, n.d., arizonahighways.com. Accessed 29 Jan. 2025.
5. "Shiva Temple, Arizona." *Peakbagger*, n.d., peakbagger.com. Accessed 29 Jan. 2025.
6. "Grand Canyon: The Trail of Time." *National Park Service*, 20 Oct. 2024, nps.gov. Accessed 29 Jan. 2025.
7. "The Trail of Time."

CHAPTER 3. THE SOUTH RIM

1. "Grand Canyon: Basic Information." *National Park Service*, 30 Nov. 2024, nps.gov. Accessed 29 Jan. 2025.

2. "Grand Canyon Visitor Center." *National Park Service*, 24 Dec. 2024, nps.gov. Accessed 29 Jan. 2025.

3. "Summer Season Tips for Visiting Grand Canyon National Park." *National Park Service*, 14 Dec. 2021, nps.gov. Accessed 29 Jan. 2025.

4. "Grand Canyon: Tusayan (Purple) Route Shuttle Bus." *National Park Service*, 1 Dec. 2024, nps.gov. Accessed 29 Jan. 2025.

5. "Rim Trail." *Grand Canyon Trust*, n.d., grandcanyontrust.org. Accessed 29 Jan. 2025.

6. Cari Morgan. "John Blaustein: Photographer and Grand Canyon Original." *OARS*, 10 July 2015, oars.com. Accessed 29 Jan. 2025.

7. "Mary Colter's Buildings at Grand Canyon." *National Park Service*, 4 Apr. 2022, nps.gov. Accessed 29 Jan. 2025.

8. Laura Allen. "A New View." *National Parks Conservation Association*, 2020, npca.org. Accessed 29 Jan. 2025.

CHAPTER 4. MAGNIFICENT VIEWS

1. "Desert View Drive." *National Park Service*, 28 Dec. 2024, nps.gov. Accessed 29 Jan. 2025.

2. "Picture Perfect." *Xanterra*, n.d., xanterra.com. Accessed 29 Jan. 2025.

3. "Grandview Point." *National Park Service*, 10 Oct. 2024, nps.gov. Accessed 29 Jan. 2025.

4. "Navajo Point." *National Park Service*, 10 Oct. 2024, nps.gov. Accessed 29 Jan. 2025.

5. "Hance Rapid." *Historical Marker Database*, 8 July 2024, hmdb.com. Accessed 29 Jan. 2025.

6. "Grand Canyon: Fees & Passes." *National Park Service*, 15 Jan. 2025, nps.gov. Accessed 29 Jan. 2025.

7. "Moran Point." *National Park Service*, 10 Oct. 2024, nps.gov. Accessed 29 Jan. 2025.

8. Ian Webster. "Value of $10,000 from 1874 to 2024." *CPI Inflation Calculator*, n.d., in2013dollars.com. Accessed 29 Jan. 2025.

9. "Grand Canyon: Hermit Road Scenic Overlooks." *National Park Service*, 1 Dec. 2024, nps.gov. Accessed 29 Jan. 2025.

10. "The Abyss – Hermits Rest (Red) Route." *National Park Service*, 1 Dec. 2024, nps.gov. Accessed 29 Jan. 2025.

11. "67 Best Sights in Grand Canyon National Park." Fodor's Travel, n.d., fodors.com. Accessed 29 Jan. 2025.

CHAPTER 5. INTO THE CANYON

1. "Grand Canyon: Day Hiking." *National Park Service*, 4 Oct. 2024, nps.gov. Accessed 30 Jan. 2025.

SOURCE NOTES CONTINUED

2. "Grand Canyon: Hiking Tips—Hike Smart." *National Park Service*, 23 Apr. 2024, nps.gov. Accessed 30 Jan. 2025.

3. "Hiking Tips—Hike Smart."

4. "Hiking Tips—Hike Smart."

5. Ellen Heyn. "Hike Bright Angel Trail." *Grand Canyon Trust*, 17 Apr. 2024, grandcanyontrust.org. Accessed 30 Jan. 2025.

6. "Mile-and-a-Half Resthouse." *National Park Service*, 13 Nov. 2024, nps.gov. Accessed 30 Jan. 2025.

7. "Bright Angel Trail." *National Park Service*, 13 Nov. 2024, nps.gov. Accessed 30 Jan. 2025.

8. "Bright Angel Trail."

9. Ash Nudd. "Best Things to Do in the Grand Canyon." *Dirt In My Shoes*, 14 Nov. 2024, dirtinmyshoes.com. Accessed 30 Jan. 2025.

10. "South Kaibab Trail." *Grand Canyon Trust*, n.d., grandcanyontrust.org. Accessed 30 Jan. 2025.

11. "South Kaibab Trail." *National Park Service*, 16 Dec. 2024, nps.gov. Accessed 30 Jan. 2025.

12. "South Kaibab Trail," *National Park Service*.

13. "Hermit Trail Grand Canyon." *National Park Service*, 12 May 2021, nps.gov. Accessed 30 Jan. 2025.

14. "Grand Canyon: Backcountry Permit." *National Park Service*, 17 Dec. 2024, nps.gov. Accessed 30 Jan. 2025.

15. Tori Peglar. "Rafting the Grand Canyon." *Grand Canyon National Park Trips*, 3 July 2023, mygrandcanyonpark.com. Accessed 30 Jan. 2025.

16. Peglar, "Rafting the Grand Canyon."

17. Peglar, "Rafting the Grand Canyon."

CHAPTER 6. THE NORTH RIM

1. "Grand Canyon: Directions and Transportation." *National Park Service*, 23 Dec. 2024, nps.gov. Accessed 30 Jan. 2025.

2. "Grand Canyon: Frequently Asked Questions." *National Park Service*, 28 Sept. 2023, nps.gov. Accessed 30 Jan. 2025.

3. "National Park Service to Reduce Bison Herd at Grand Canyon." *National Park Service*, 6 Sept. 2017, nps.gov. Accessed 30 Jan. 2025.

4. "100 Bison Successfully Relocated from North Rim." *National Park Service*, 16 Sept. 2024, nps.gov. Accessed 30 Jan. 2025.

5. "Grand Canyon: Birds." *National Park Service*, 30 Sept. 2020, nps.gov. Accessed 30 Jan. 2025.

6. "Rainbow Rim Trail #10." *MTB Project*, n.d., mtbproject.com. Accessed 30 Jan. 2025.

7. "Cape Royal Road." *National Park Service*, 1 Nov. 2024, nps.gov. Accessed 30 Jan. 2025.

8. Stefanie Payne. "About Me." *Stefanie Payne*, n.d., stefaniepayne.com. Accessed 30 Jan. 2025.

9. "North Kaibab Trail." *National Park Service*, 18 Oct. 2024, nps.gov. Accessed 30 Jan. 2025.

CHAPTER 7. THE PEOPLE OF THE GRAND CANYON

1. "Grand Canyon: Associated Tribes." *National Park Service*, 31 Dec. 2024, nps.gov. Accessed 30 Jan. 2025.

2. "The Hualapai Tribe History." *Grand Canyon West*, n.d., grandcanyonwest.com. Accessed 30 Jan. 2025.

3. "Skywalk at Eagle Point." *Grand Canyon West*, n.d., grandcanyonwest.com. Accessed 30 Jan. 2025.

4. Jeremy Hobson. "The Havasupai Tribe's Long Connection to the Canyon's Red Rocks." *WBUR*, 13 Aug. 2019, wbur.org. Accessed 30 Jan. 2025.

5. Sarah Gerke and Paul Hirt. "Havasupai Reservation." *Nature, Culture and History at the Grand Canyon*, n.d., grcahistory.org. Accessed 30 Jan. 2025.

6. "Zipline at Hualapai Point." *Grand Canyon West*, n.d., grandcanyonwest.com. Accessed 30 Jan. 2025.

7. "Havasupai Indian Reservation." *National Park Service*, 29 Jan. 2025, nps.gov. Accessed 30 Jan. 2025.

8. "Mule Train Delivery." *USPS Postal Facts*, n.d., facts.usps.com. Accessed 30 Jan. 2025.

9. "Havasupai Indian Reservation."

10. "Supai." *Visit Arizona*, n.d., visitarizona.com. Accessed 30 Jan. 2025.

11. Teresa Bitler. "A Guide to Visiting Havasu Falls." *Visit Arizona*, n.d., visitarizona.com. Accessed 30 Jan. 2025.

CHAPTER 8. STAYING SAFE

1. "Grand Canyon: Emergency Services." *National Park Service*, 30 Aug. 2024, nps.gov. Accessed 30 Jan. 2025.

2. "Grand Canyon: Weather and Climate." *National Park Service*, 5 June 2020, nps.gov. Accessed 30 Jan. 2025.

3. "Weather and Climate."

4. "Weather and Climate."

5. Morgan Lee and Brittany Peterson. "A Search Ended in Heartbreak." *Associated Press*, 3 Sept. 2024, apnews.com. Accessed 30 Jan. 2025.

6. Lee and Peterson, "A Search Ended in Heartbreak."

7. "Grand Canyon: Rattlesnakes." *National Park Service*, 26 Feb. 2022, nps.gov. Accessed 30 Jan. 2025.

INDEX

Anthony, Harold Elmer, 23
Antiquities Act of 1906, 12
Ashurst, Henry Fountain, 13

biking, 6, 26, 29, 31, 40, 43, 47, 57, 72
boating, 6, 10, 33, 63–65, 80, 96

camping, 10, 57, 61, 68, 87–89
Cárdenas, García López de, 6–7
Colorado River, 6, 7, 8, 10, 11, 19–21, 30, 33, 37, 38, 42–43, 47, 49–50, 58, 60, 61, 63–65, 73, 76, 80, 96
Colter, Mary, 33–34, 37
Coronado, Francisco Vázquez de, 6

Desert View Watchtower, 37, 40, 43, 45, 75, 99
dining, 10, 26, 29, 31–32, 69, 70–71
Dutton, Clarence, 22

Ford, Gerald, 13

geology, 4, 16–25, 44, 52, 58
    Grand Canyon Supergroup, 44
    temples, 22–23, 25, 42, 50, 60
Grand Canyon Forest Reserve, 11
Grand Canyon National Game Preserve, 11
Grand Canyon Railway, 8–9, 10, 26, 28, 32
Grand Canyon Skywalk, 81, 82
Grand Canyon Star Party, 35
Grand Canyon Village, 31–33, 40, 46, 47, 99
Great Unconformity, 20

Harrison, Benjamin, 11
Havasu Canyon, 85–87, 96
Havasupai Gardens, 57
Hayes, Rutherford B., 86
helicopters, 78, 80, 88, 96

Hermits Rest, 31, 34
hiking, 26, 28, 31, 32, 34, 42, 47, 52–61, 63, 72, 73, 76–77, 87–88, 93, 96–97, 99
Hopi House, 34

Indigenous peoples, 6, 13–14, 34, 55–56, 73, 75, 78–81, 83–88, 95
    Apache, 14
    Diné (Navajo), 14
    Havasupai, 14, 57, 78, 85–88, 95–96
    Hopi, 6, 14, 34, 84
    Hualapai, 14, 78–81, 83–84
    Mojave, 84
    Southern Paiute, 14
    Zuni, 14
Ives, Joseph Christmas, 8

Kaibab National Forest, 73
Kolb, Ellsworth, 10, 33
Kolb, Emery, 10, 33
Kolb Studio, 10, 33

lodging, 10, 26, 31–33, 47, 68–71, 76, 81, 87–88, 93
    El Tovar Hotel, 32–33, 47
    Grand Canyon Lodge, 68–71, 76
    Grand Canyon Railway Hotel, 32
    Phantom Ranch, 93
Lookout Studio, 34, 36

Mather, Stephen Tyng, 29
Mexican-American War, 7–8
mining, 8, 13, 34, 42, 81
Moran, Thomas, 44–45
mules, 6, 42, 47, 54, 55, 61, 62–63, 76, 77, 87

National Park Service (NPS), 16, 29, 52, 54, 57, 58, 59–60, 65, 78, 86–87, 90
Nickerson, Andrew, 95–96
Nickerson, Chenoa, 95–96
North Rim, 57, 61, 66–77, 94, 99

park passes, 43, 68
permits, 61, 65, 87
photography, 10, 31, 33, 34, 35, 40, 45, 75, 82, 99
Powell, John Wesley, 49

Roosevelt, Theodore, 6, 11–12, 13, 32–33

safety, 52–55, 72, 73, 76–77, 86, 90–99
scenic drives, 38–50, 70, 73–76
    Arizona State Route 67, 70, 73
    Cape Royal Road, 73–76
    Desert View Drive, 38–46
    Hermit Road, 46–50
scenic overlooks, 26, 29–31, 38–50, 58–60, 72–76, 77, 81
    Abyss, 48
    Cape Royal, 75–76
    Cedar Ridge, 59–60
    Coconino Overlook, 77
    Crazy Jug Point, 73
    Eagle Point, 81–82, 84
    Grandview Point, 42
    Guano Point, 81, 83
    Hopi Point, 49–50
    Lipan Point, 43–44
    Mather Point, 29–31
    Moran Point, 44
    Navajo Point, 42–43
    Ooh Aah Point, 58–59
    Pima Point, 49
    Pipe Creek Vista, 41–42
    Point Imperial, 73–74
    Powell Point, 49
    Shoshone Point, 46
    Skeleton Point, 60
    Trailview Overlook, 47
    Yaki Point, 45
shuttle buses, 28–29, 31, 32, 40–41, 43, 45, 46, 57, 81, 99
South Rim, 9, 10, 14, 24, 25, 26–37, 38–50, 55–63, 66, 68, 75, 76, 77, 87
Supai Village, 87, 88

trails, 24, 26, 29, 31, 32, 34, 41, 42, 46, 47, 54–61, 72, 73, 75–77, 86, 87–89, 93, 99
    Bright Angel Point Trail, 76
    Bright Angel Trail, 47, 55–58, 60
    Grandview Trail, 42
    Hermit Trail, 34, 60–61
    North Kaibab Trail, 77
    Rainbow Rim Trail, 72
    Rim Trail, 31, 34, 41
    South Kaibab Trail, 58–60
    Trail of Time, 24

Underwood, Gilbert Stanley, 70
UNESCO, 14–15

visitor centers, 28–29, 31, 68, 97, 99

Walhalla Glades Pueblo, 74–75
waterfalls, 21, 88–89, 96
weather, 40, 50, 68, 73, 93–97, 99
West Rim, 80–89
wildlife, 11, 13, 23, 35, 36, 41–42, 43, 61, 66, 68, 71, 72, 73, 86, 97–98, 99
Williams, Arizona, 9, 10, 32
Wilson, Woodrow, 13

Yavapai Geology Museum, 24, 25

ABOUT THE AUTHOR

ASHLEY STORM

Ashley Storm is a writer and lawyer living in Kentucky with her husband, three mischievous cats, and a flock of bossy backyard chickens. She has written more than 30 books for children and young adults.